Crocodiles

Hannah Cole

This book belongs to:

OXFORD
UNIVERSITY PRESS

Great Clarendon Street, Oxford OX2 6DP
Oxford University Press is a department of the University of Oxford.
It furthers the University's objective of excellence in research, scholarship,
and education by publishing worldwide in

Oxford New York

Auckland Cape Town Dar es Salaam Hong Kong Karachi
Kuala Lumpur Madrid Melbourne Mexico City Nairobi
New Delhi Shanghai Taipei Toronto

With offices in

Argentina Austria Brazil Chile Czech Republic France Greece
Guatemala Hungary Italy Japan Poland Portugal Singapore
South Korea Switzerland Thailand Turkey Ukraine Vietnam

This edition 2009

British Library Cataloguing in Publication Data

Data available

ISBN: 978-0-19-911926-4

1 3 5 7 9 10 8 6 4 2

Printed in China
Paper used in the production of this book is a natural,
recyclable product made from wood grown in sustainable forests.
The manufacturing process conforms to the environmental
regulations of the country of origin.

Contents

▶ Crocodiles are good at staying alive

Crocodiles have been around for a long time. There were crocodiles on the earth 200 million years ago.

That was when there were still dinosaurs, long, long before people.

Dinosaurs died out, but not crocodiles. Crocodiles are good at staying alive because they are fast and strong and sensible.

Crocodiles are fast

Crocodiles can jump and run. They can jump out of the water so fast that they can catch a bird as it goes by.

They like to lie down, but they can stand up and run fast if they need to.

When a crocodile sees food, it does not rush. It waits. It is so still that the food does not see it. On land, it looks like an old log.

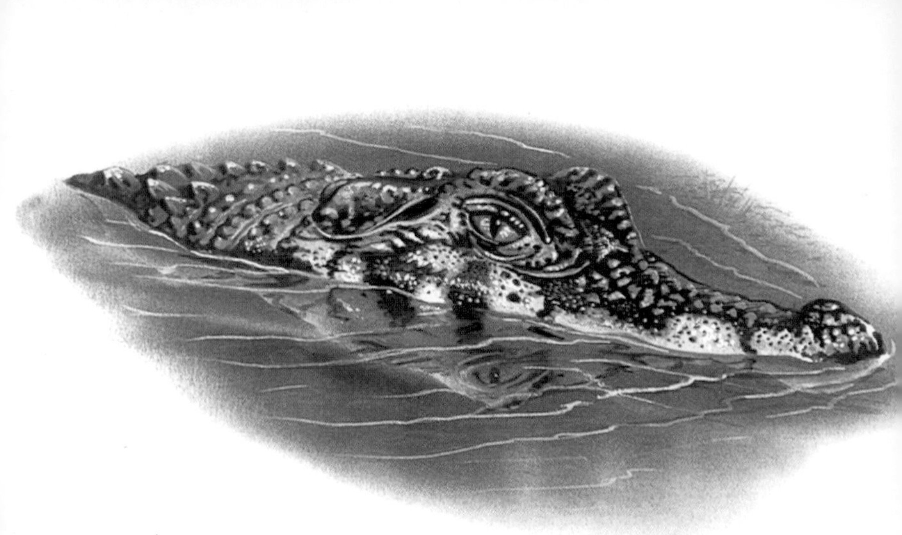

caiman

In water, only its eyes and its nose show. When the food is near the crocodile, then the crocodile can be fast.

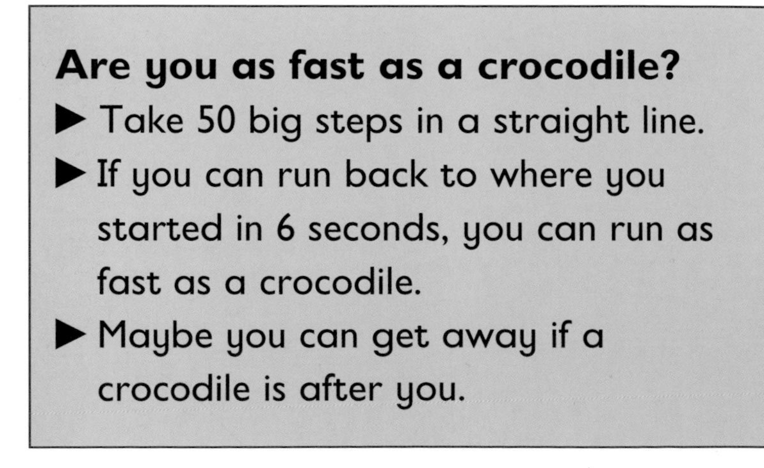

Are you as fast as a crocodile?

- Take 50 big steps in a straight line.
- If you can run back to where you started in 6 seconds, you can run as fast as a crocodile.
- Maybe you can get away if a crocodile is after you.

A crocodile moves its tail from side to side to swim along.

It can swim fast enough to catch a fish.

Can you?

Nile crocodile

Crocodiles are strong

A crocodile mouth is strong for shutting. If it shuts on your leg the bones will break.

A crocodile mouth is not strong for opening. A rubber band can stop it opening (but it's hard to put it on).

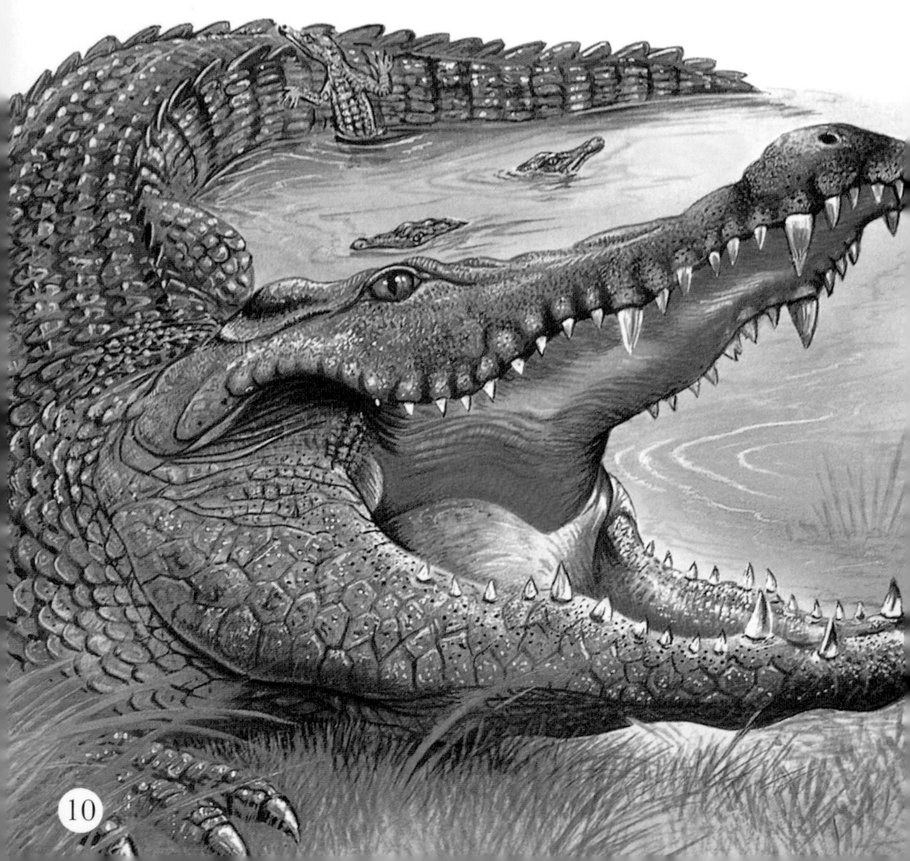

A crocodile stops its food from getting away. It holds the food under water till it is dead.

If a cow comes to the water for a drink, the crocodile will bite its nose and pull the cow into the water.

Nile crocodile and wildebeest

Crocodiles are sensible

Crocodiles live in warm places where there is shallow water. They like lakes, ponds, and slow rivers.

If it gets too hot, they stay in the water.

If it gets too dry, they hide in a hole and wait for rain.

A mother crocodile can take her babies over land to find new water.

You were born alive, but crocodile babies start as eggs. The crocodile mother makes a nest of sand or dirt. She lays about 50 eggs and covers them up. The eggs are not hard like hens' eggs. They are soft like rubber.

The crocodile baby grows inside its egg. When its mother hears the baby calling, she picks up the egg in her mouth. Very gently, she squashes the egg so that the baby can get out. She puts the baby in the water.

Nile crocodile and her babies

A baby crocodile is good food for birds and turtles and otters, so all the crocodiles help to look after the babies. They roar if they see danger and chase away the enemies.

But if some babies are eaten up, there are still lots left.

Grown-up people stop growing, but crocodiles go on growing till they die. Some crocodiles live till they are 100 years old. Some crocodiles grow till they are five metres long, as long as a big camper van.

Did you know...

One crocodile grew longer than the front of a full size football goal.

What crocodiles eat

Crocodiles don't eat fruit or vegetables. Small crocodiles eat small animals, like insects and crabs, birds and fish. Small crocodiles won't eat you.

Did you know...

As well as meat, crocodiles eat hard things like stones and bits of metal. Maybe the stones help to mash up the food inside the crocodile.

black caiman

Big crocodiles eat cows and sheep, zebras and hippos. If they want to eat a very big animal, lots of crocodiles help to pull it into bits.

If you go where there are crocodiles, try not to look like food. Don't put your arms or legs in the water. Don't ever feed a crocodile. It can't tell which is food and which is hand.

How many meals do you eat every day? Big crocodiles eat one meal in a week. If you have no food, you will die after a few weeks. Crocodiles can last for more than a year with no food.

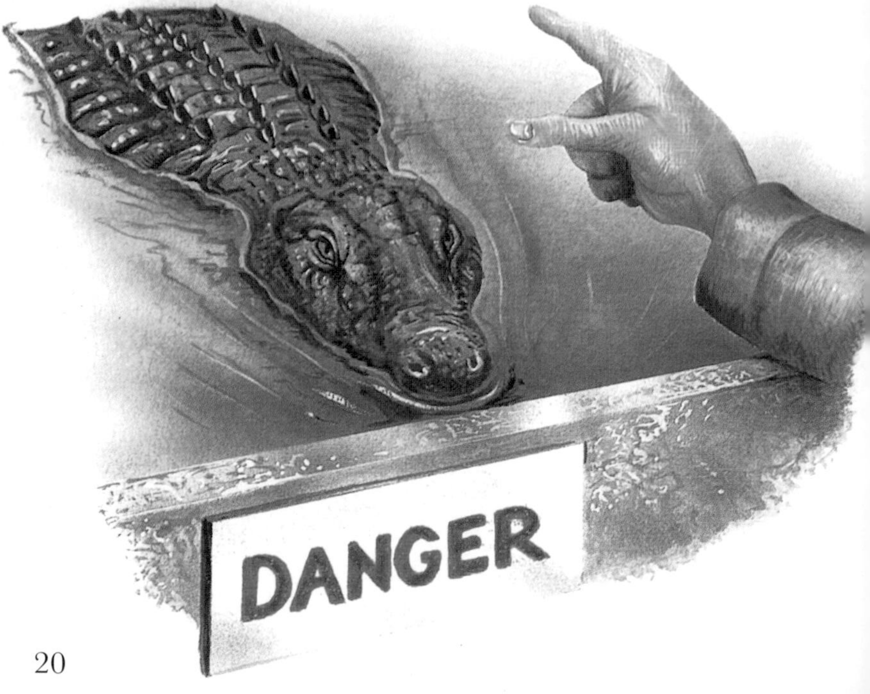

How crocodiles eat

Crocodiles are good at staying alive because they always have lots of teeth to catch food with.

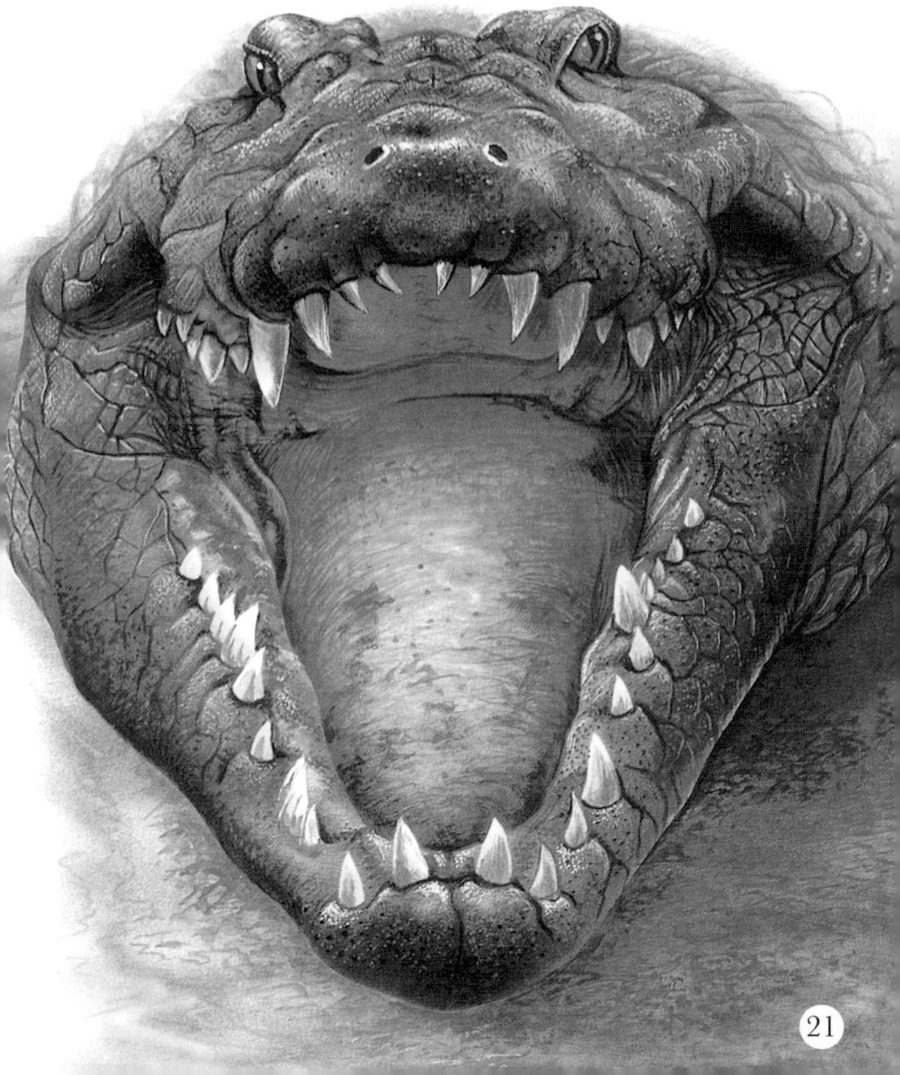

You started with no teeth at all, **but crocodile babies start with a mouth full of teeth.**

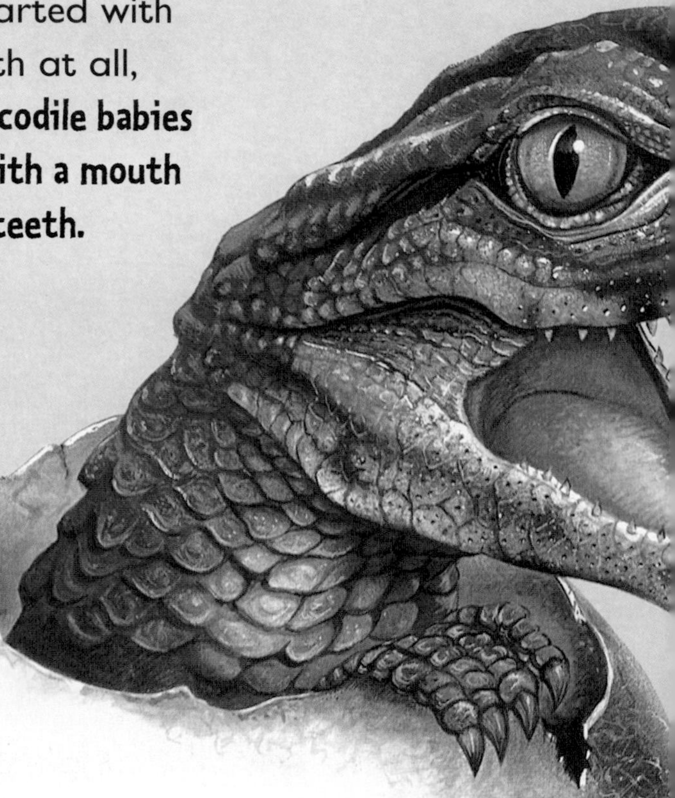

People have two sets of teeth: first baby teeth and then big teeth. **Some crocodiles have 45 sets of new teeth.**

How many teeth have you got? **Some crocodiles have 100 teeth.**

You may lose your
teeth when you are old,
**but when crocodile teeth fall out,
there are new teeth under the old ones.
Crocodiles keep on getting new teeth.**

**Crocodiles don't need biting teeth
like our sharp front teeth.
They don't need chewing teeth like
our flat back teeth.
Crocodiles have pointed teeth,
to hold on to their food.**

If a crocodile wants to eat you, it holds on to your leg so you can't run away. It pulls till your leg comes off.

It swallows your leg all in one go.
If a crocodile gets you, be quick.
Hurry before it pulls off your leg.
Hurry before it pulls you under water.
Hurry up and make it let go.

The only way to make it let go is to hurt it. A crocodile has strong skin, so the best way to hurt it is to poke it in the eye or poke it in the nose. If you poke it hard, it **may** let go.

But only hurt a crocodile if the crocodile is hurting you. That's fair.

How crocodiles die

Some crocodiles are kept on farms. People eat their meat and make things out of their skins.

Some people kill crocodiles by mistake.

They may want more land for farms and houses, and when they make the wet land dry, the crocodiles can't live there.

They may run them over with their cars.

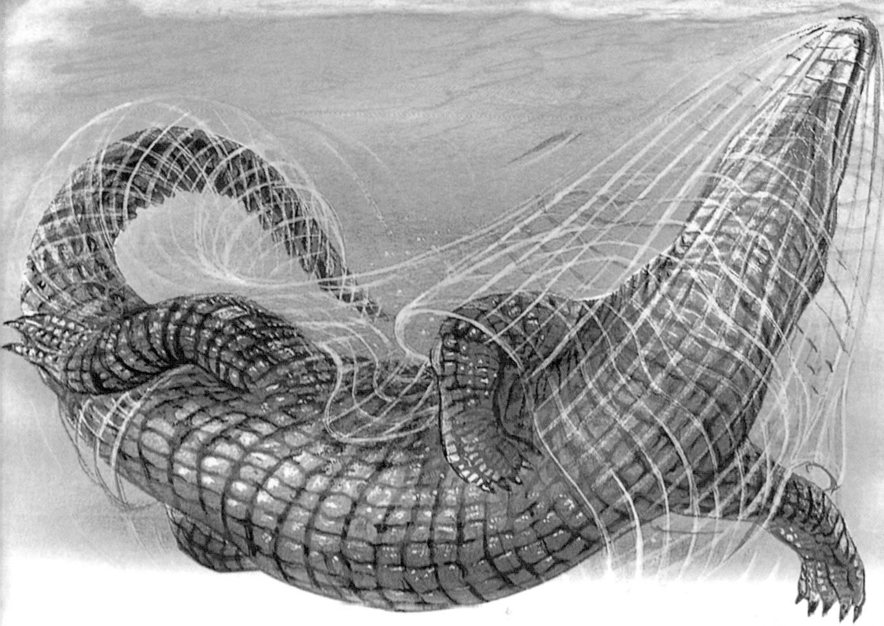

They may tangle a crocodile in a fishing net so that it can't come up to get air. It can stay under water for longer than you can, but in the end, it drowns.

In the time of the dinosaurs, crocodiles were very good at staying alive. It's harder for them now.

There were crocodiles on the earth 200 million years ago. Do you think there will still be crocodiles 200 million years from now?

In the crocodile family

crocodiles

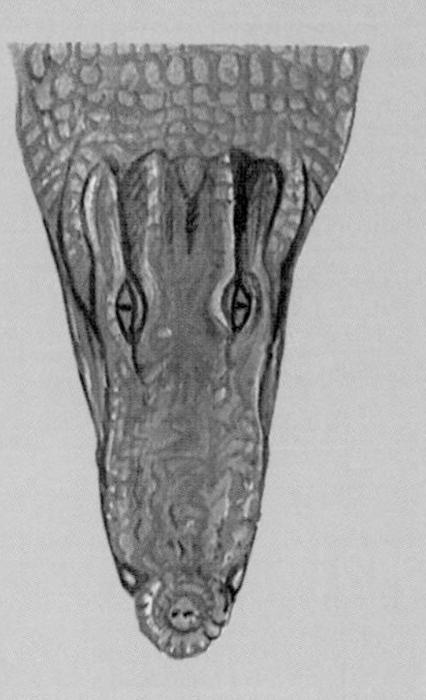

Crocodiles are the ones with one big tooth sticking up on each side. They have pointed noses.

alligators

Alligators have square noses. You can't see that big tooth because it hides inside the mouth.

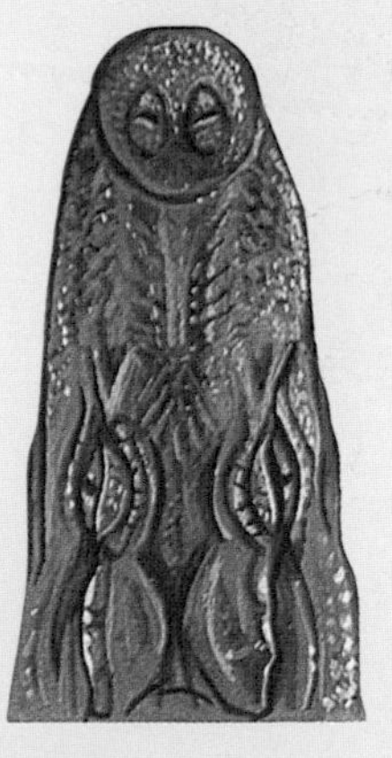

caimans

Caimans (or caymans) are the ones you are most likely to see in a zoo. They are like small alligators.

gavials

Gavials (or gharials) are the ones with very long thin noses.

Crocodiles, alligators, caimans and gavials are all in the crocodile family.

OXFORD

WILD READS

WILD READS will help your child develop a love of reading and a lasting curiosity about our world. See the websites and places to visit below to learn more about crocodiles.

Crocodiles

WEBSITES

http://www.bbc.co.uk/cbbc/wild/amazinganimals/

http://kids.nationalgeographic.com/

PLACES TO VISIT

West Midlands Safari Park
http://www.wmsp.co.uk/index.php

London Zoo
http://www.zsl.org/

Amazon World, Isle of Wight
http://www.amazonworld.co.uk/